AF479837

THIS IS GOOD NEWS

Written by Kathryn Binger   Illustrated by Tiffany Cipriano Carvalho

In the beginning, God made man and woman. They lived in a beautiful garden called Eden. In the garden they walked and talked with God every day. They were like God, and God was one with them.

Then, man and woman disobeyed God. When they did this wrong thing, they could suddenly see that they had no clothes. They quickly made some clothes and tried to hide from God. They felt dirty inside, and the inside of them died.

To protect the man and woman from other things in the Garden, God made them leave the Garden.

When they left the Garden they could not walk and talk with God like they used to. Bad things happened because of the man and woman's disobedience to God.
They died on the inside, they felt lost all of their life, and eventually their bodies died too.

But, God had a plan!
He started a family through a man
named Abraham.

God promised to one day send a Man to save all humanity from dying. That man would come from the family God started. God called this family ISRAEL.

THIS IS JESUS AS MESSIAH

The Man God promised to send is named Jesus.
Jesus is the Son of God and He is God. Jesus was born as a human baby,
and grew up as a human Man, but He existed before
He was born as a Man. Jesus came as God walking on the earth again.
When Jesus was 33 years old, He died on the cross.
He shed all of His blood and His body was broken on the cross.
Then He was buried.
Then Jesus was brought back to life by Holy Spirit,
Who is also God. Jesus died, was buried, and rose again to get rid of the
bad things that happened when man and woman disobeyed God in the
Garden. He made the way for the inside of us to live again.
Now we can have peace with God.

YOU ARE NOT DIRTY ON THE INSIDE. ANYMORE!!
THIS IS JESUS AS HIGH PRIEST

After Jesus made the way for us to live again, He went back up to Heaven. Jesus took the blood He shed on the cross up into Heaven to give us eternal life.

Jesus is now sitting on a throne in Heaven, next to God the Father. Jesus prays for us. Jesus' blood always says that we are not dirty on the inside anymore. His blood brought us close to God again.

Now we can walk and talk with God like man and woman did in the Garden. When Jesus went to Heaven, He sent Holy Spirit, the One who brought Him back to life, down to the earth. When we receive Holy Spirit, we are filled with God's power.

THIS IS JESUS AS BRIDEGROOM

One day soon, Jesus will come back to the earth. We will know that Jesus is back when we see the sky split open like a wave when it hits a rock.

We get to hope in the Day Jesus is coming back.

The more we hope in that Day, the more we become like Jesus. And on that Day everyone who has been hoping in Jesus' return will be called Jesus' bride.

When we see Jesus split the sky, we will become completely like Him. When we think and talk about Jesus' return, we grow in purity.

When we believe into Jesus Christ as Lord and Savior, God gives us the perfect gift of GRACE.

Grace is God's power to save us. Any good or right thing we do is done because of grace.

Grace is God's power to save us. What have we been saved from? We have been saved from all of the bad things that happened when man and woman disobeyed God in the Garden of Eden.

When we are saved, we become full of God's righteousness.

What is righteousness?
Righteousness is us having God's perfect character inside of us.
Righteousness is us being like God.
This is just how the man and woman in the Garden were before they disobeyed God, because they were one with God.

When we become one with God again, we are brought into union with God.
Us being one with God again, having union with Him, is the reason why Jesus came the first time.

This union with God causes us to
produce good fruit,
but not like oranges or apples.

This fruit is every good and right
thing we do in being like God.

If you want to be one
with God, you can give
your life to Him.

All you have to do
is believe that Jesus
did come, He did die,
He did rise again,
He did send Holy Spirit
to us, and He will
come back again.

Simply say to Jesus,

'Jesus, I believe that You came, You died, You rose again,
You sent Holy Spirit, and You will come back again.
I am sorry for all the wrong things I have done.
I turn away from the wrong things, and give my life to You.
My life does not belong to me anymore.
My life belongs to You. You are my Lord and my Savior.
I believe in You, Jesus.
In Jesus' name. Amen.'

Your life now belongs to God and you are in union with Him!
Welcome to God's family!

THE TWELVE PILLARS OF THE GOSPEL
PURE

Each page of this book explains one of the twelve pillars of the Gospel of Jesus Christ.

Page 1: 'THE GARDEN'

Page 2: 'THE FALL'

Page 3: 'CONSEQUENCES'

Page 4: 'ISRAEL'

Page 5: 'MESSIAH'

Page 6: 'HIGH PRIEST'

Page 7: 'BRIDEGROOM'

Page 8: 'GRACE'

Page 9: 'SALVATION'

Page 10: 'RIGHTEOUSNESS'

Page 11: 'UNION'

Page 12: 'FRUIT'

Author's note:

Parents, you are called to be the disciplers of your children.
As you learn and grow in the Good News, invite
your children to grow with you.
I love you and your children, and I cannot
wait to hear the testimonies that come from you reading
this book with your family.
Maranatha! Come Lord Jesus!

Each page of this book explains one of the twelve pillars of the Gospel of Jesus Christ.

Page 1: 'THE GARDEN'

Page 2: 'THE FALL'

Page 3: 'CONSEQUENCES'

Page 4: 'ISRAEL'

Page 5: 'MESSIAH'

Page 6: 'HIGH PRIEST'

Page 7: 'BRIDEGROOM'

Page 8: 'GRACE'

Page 9: 'SALVATION'

Page 10: 'RIGHTEOUSNESS'

Page 11: 'UNION'

Page 12: 'FRUIT'

Author's note:

Parents, you are called to be the disciplers of your children.
As you learn and grow in the Good News, invite
your children to grow with you.
I love you and your children, and I cannot
wait to hear the testimonies that come from you reading
this book with your family.
Maranatha! Come Lord Jesus!